Behind Media

Radio

Catherine Chambers

Heinemann Library
Chicago, Illinois

Designed by Paul Davies and Associates
Originated by Ambassador Litho Ltd.
Printed in Hong Kong/China

05 04 03 02 01
10 9 8 7 6 5 4 3 2 1

Library of Congress Cataloging-in-Publication Data
Chambers, Catherine, 1966-
    Radio / Catherine Chambers.
        p. cm. -- (Behind media)
    Includes bibliographical references and index.
    ISBN 1-58810-034-0 (library binding)
    1. Radio broadcasting--Juvenile literature. [1. Radio broadcasting.] I. Title. II. Series.

PN1991.57 .C46 2001
384.54--dc21

                                                        00-046164

Acknowledgments
The author and publishers are grateful to the following for permission to reproduce copyright material: Action-Plus/Glyn Kirk, p. 22; Arena, pp. 4, 26, 30; Capital FM Radio, pp. 15, 17; Corbis/Christopher Cormack, p. 32; The Purcell Team, p. 6; Bob Rowan, p. 13; Staffan Widstrand, p. 24; David Swindells, p. 40; Eliot Stein, p. 45; Environmental Images/Michael Marchant, p. 37; John Mead/Science Photo Library, p. 34; Panos Pictures, p. 9; Crispin Hughes, p. 8; Clive Shirley, p. 21; Chris Stowers, p. 38; Popperfoto, p. 41; Press Association/Neil Munns, p. 19; Radio 4ZzZ, p. 10; Redferns/Suzi Gibbons, p. 19; Rex Features, p. 14; Science & Society Picture Library/Science Museum, p. 44; Stay Still Ltd/Sven Arnstein, p. 39; Stone, p. 42; Sylvia Pitcher Photo Library, p. 11; Telegraph Colour Library, pp. 16, 29; The Stock Market, p. 7; Tommy Hindley/Professional Sport, p. 5.

Cover photograph reproduced with permission of Telegraph Colour Library.

Our thanks to Robert McLeish for his comments in the preparation of this book.

Every effort has been made to contact copyright holders of any material reproduced in this book. Any omissions will be rectified in subsequent printings if notice is given to the publisher.

Some words are shown in bold, **like this.** You can find out what they mean by looking in the glossary.

Contents

The Waves at Daybreak

Getting It off the Ground

The Show Begins

All in a Day's Work

Behind the Mike

Turn on the Radio

The Waves at Daybreak

Why Radio?

About 80 years ago, switches were clicked, knobs were turned, and like magic, plain wooden boxes suddenly sparked to life. At first muffled and crackled, real voices crossed invisible waves and entered the heart of the home. In a short amount of time, radio became an entertainer, an educator, and a companion for millions of people all over the world.

Radio stations around the world wake people every morning with news, views, music, and chat. This book aims to take you through an early-morning radio show, explaining how it is put together and broadcast to a local community. Other shows and aspects of radio broadcasting will be discussed as well, to provide a wider picture of this medium.

*DJs, newscasters, weather reporters, and **continuity** announcers all have to interact with perfect timing to create entertaining and interesting programs. Often, a newscaster or special guest will record in a studio separate from the main presenter.*

What is the attraction?

A radio can be portable and inexpensive. It can be listened to quietly through headphones, or it can be enjoyed by a whole roomful of people. A person can drive and listen to the radio at the same time. You can walk, work, and listen, too. Recent research has found that you can even study with your favorite radio station on, and it may actually help you!

Radio stations can be tuned in at any time of the day or night—there is always something to keep a listener company. He or she can even tune in a foreign station and help brush up on world languages. Without pictures, the listener's imagination can run wild.

These are just some of the reasons why Americans listen to the radio for an average of three hours every day. And it is why the United States now has over 14,000 radio stations. Worldwide, the scale of radio is enormous. UNESCO (United Nations Educational, Scientific, and Cultural Organization) estimates that there are 2.4 billion radio sets throughout the world. Of all the thousands of stations around the world, local stations are considered to be the heart and soul of the radio broadcasting industry, bringing community happenings into the home and workplace.

Specialty stations offer specialty news. Sports stations provide the latest information on teams, players, transfers, the financial side of sports, trials, trophies, and gossip. These stations also use guest presenters, such as John McEnroe for tennis.

Who makes it all happen?

Radio personalities are the most hidden of the media world. The listener rarely sees the people who create the programs, and rarely does he or she recognize them when they pick up their trophies at broadcasting awards ceremonies. However, behind the scenes, a team of **producers, directors,** production assistants, **studio managers,** editors, and technicians mold voices and noises into shape. This book will look at the functions of many of those involved in radio production, the techniques they use, and the workings of a recording studio.

Will it last?

Since the 1950s, radio has met with fierce competition from television. When TV first appeared, radio **ratings** plummeted and producers were forced to think of new ways to attract an audience. Teenagers came to the rescue with their thirst for popular music and culture, and thus the pop station was born. Later, we will see how radio is holding up against the latest media development—the Internet.

What's the Story?

The expression **"drive time** is **prime time"** refers to the time between 6:30 A.M. and 9:30 A.M., when many people listen to news and talk shows while they drive to work. Every day countless radio and television stations compete for their share of the early morning audience. Despite the popularity of television, radio continues to be popular in its own right and does have a lot to offer.

Morning glory

If you flip through the radio stations around breakfast time, you will find a great range of early morning shows. In the last 30 years, these shows have established a strong identity in the face of competition from breakfast television. While television provides a very accessible account of news, commentary, and entertainment, it tends to stress national and international events. These are often of greater visual impact than the smaller local stories and news. Natural disasters, war, accidents, crime, political scandals, and glitzy awards ceremonies are all standard television material. For the early-morning commuter, however, they are only background noise to the more important task ahead—getting to work on time, armed with enough information about what is going on locally and in the world at large. It is time to tune in to the radio.

On the pulse

Radio can provide all the information people getting ready to face the day require: national and international headlines, regional news items, financial updates, and frequent time checks. National and regional weather forecasts, and often traffic news, help the traveling listeners prepare for the conditions they may encounter.

Most traffic news is supplied by reporters using helicopters to track trouble spots. Together with information from the emergency services and road maintenance companies, they keep the commuter well informed. Many traffic bulletins include suggested alternate routes to avoid construction or congestion.

*Prime-time hours are defined through extensive market research undertaken by broadcasters and **ratings** companies. They use a variety of techniques to gauge the listening habits of radio fans.*

Radio manages to communicate information in a few set **formats.** Presentation ranges from pop shows interrupted by quick news bulletins, to straightforward news summaries followed by lengthy analysis. Some stations are known for their serious content and tone, while others pick out off-beat stories and present them in an amusing way. You can pick your station to suit your mood as well as your needs. On commercial stations, advertisements and **jingles** are played between news stories or songs.

Out of the ark

In the last two decades, early-morning music and talk shows have adopted the "zoo formula"—a crazy concoction of lively presenters, co-presenters, and media personalities. The contents include very informal chat with listeners about bizarre subjects, wild antics in the studio—and of course the occasional news bulletin. This formula began in the United States and has spread to many corners of the world. While it is still very popular, one ex-prime-time presenter, Noel Edmonds, has said of the zoo formula, ". . . I think that radio is an intimate medium from one person to another. You can get the feeling that if there is a group of people on the radio they are having a better time than you are, and there are in[side]-jokes that you don't understand that unsettle you." Whatever your preference, you can find something on the radio.

Early radio

✿ In the 1920s, **producers** realized that listening to the news was a much quicker and more convenient way of catching up on events than reading the newspaper.

✿ In 1922, Radio 2LO became the British Broadcasting Company's first London station. One of the first items was the news. It was read twice, once at normal speed and once very slowly. Each news item was separated from the next by a chime of tubular bells that was supposed to sound like a chiming clock.

Wide Horizons

Radio is a web of information that spirals outward from local stations to international **networks.** It has long been used to educate at both levels and has proven extremely useful in many different parts of the world.

Listen and learn

Radio has always been used to inform and educate both adults and young people. In many areas, its role for the young has been largely to supplement classroom teaching, often using plays, music, stories, and games to encourage learning. In more remote parts of the world, radio has been used for communicating the mainstream school syllabus. Some local radio stations serve ethnic minority communities, providing news and entertainment in a variety of languages. They have contacts worldwide, tapping into reports from the "home" country and other parts of the world where people of the same community have settled.

In rural areas, local radio helps farmers to keep up with developments in agriculture. Internationally, the BBC World Service's Farming World *program discusses global agricultural techniques. Many stations are now linked to websites so that hard-working farmers can study the information in their own time.*

In a more tragic setting, radio is playing a big part in rehabilitating Rwanda's children following the massacres in 1998. These left many children without parents and many households with an older brother or sister in charge of younger siblings. In 2000, the Rwandan government and the charity War Child worked to provide a radio service that aims to educate the children of Rwanda whose schools have not yet been rebuilt, focusing especially on the young caregivers. These students will be given not only mainstream education, but also information on childcare, immunization programs, and farming techniques—extremely important for these family providers, who are really children themselves. War Child is providing 65,000 wind-up radios, which work without batteries or electricity (see also page 45).

*One of the most successful and longest-running education projects has been Australia's School of the Air, which operates in very inaccessible, sparsely populated rural areas. With regular broadcast lessons and tutorials on **two-way radio,** farming families have been able to educate their children. In recent years, the Internet has supplemented these lessons with e-mail communication.*

Radio sets around the world

The table below shows the number of radio sets used in different countries. It is not always necessarily true that richer nations have more radio sets per person. Television is usually the preferred medium in wealthier countries.

There is a lot of interdependence among local, national, and international radio broadcasting, but the quality and variety of information used depends a lot on how the station is financed.

Country	Population (in millions)	No. of radio sets on average
Australia	19	1.4 per person
France	59	1 per person
India	944	1.2 per 10 people
Italy	57	8.8 per 10 people
Nigeria	115	1 per 5 people
U.K.	59	1.4 per person
U.S.	275	More than 2 per person

Radio power

Many of the world's most powerful nations broadcast to as many countries as possible through publicly funded international stations. The Voice of America is the foreign broadcasting arm of the United States, and the BBC World Service is that of the United Kingdom. Some of their programs inform listeners about news and events in the U.S. or U.K. and provide an analysis of world events from their own point of view. Others give listeners an insight into projects and developments, both at home and in other corners of the world.

Getting It off the Ground

Paying the Piper

How does a new program get off the ground? First there is the nitty-gritty subject of money. Every program has to be financed, which means that it must have a proven need and a target audience before it will find any backers. Radio programs can be funded in a number of ways, including commercial advertising, license fees, subscriptions, and government funding.

Who is listening?

Densely populated urban areas spawn a large number of radio stations with a huge following. There is a lot of competition for both listeners and **revenue.** Rural areas, being sparsely populated, generate less revenue than urban areas and can sustain only a few local stations.

Bananas and microphones do go together—at least in Queensland, Australia, they do. They represent the state's controversial 25-year-old radio station "Triple-Z." It has financed itself by various means, including a "Zedbubble Market Day" and this message to encourage sponsorship: "Zed has over 100 dedicated volunteers working their butts off so we can stay on air."

Many costs of running stations are roughly the same for all areas, depending on the size and number of studios rather than their location. These costs include power, equipment, licenses, telephone, and satellite links—basically, all the required equipment and services that are bought outright or leased. The salaries of technical personnel are also similar for all stations. **Prime-time** radio presenters, on the other hand, can command huge fees, especially those employed at national radio stations located in major cities. Studio space in cities can also be expensive.

Finding the money

Advertisements account for most of a local commercial station's revenue. A lot of advertising time is bought by local retailers and service industries. Station advertising representatives (reps) also negotiate with national advertising companies and promotions departments of multi-national companies to sell **air time.** However, while these national **network** contracts can be lucrative, they must not overwhelm local advertising. A local station cannot afford to lose its loyal listener base. Both local and national commercial stations lure sponsorship for individual programs or even small **slots** within them, such as contests, as well as for the station as a whole. Internet radio is now attracting huge amounts of investment. In May 2000, U.S. Digital Radio, based in Maryland, received $41 million to develop its worldwide service.

Capturing the audience

The formula for radio shows is continually being re-evaluated, especially the prime-time breakfast show. There are often slight changes in presentation or presenters that freshen the image without costing a great deal or losing the regular, dedicated listener. These changes are often timed for the beginning of the new year; the birth of the millennium saw a huge number of revamped radio shows, but when a new program completely replaces an old one, it usually means that the slot, or even the whole station, has suffered a drop in **ratings.**

A small rural station like this may have smaller studio space and staff costs than a city station, but it also generates far less income.

Ratings affect the profitability of all radio stations, regardless of how they are financed. For example, some governments support national radio stations, solely or partially, by collecting taxes or imposing a license fee, but they cannot justify an increase in taxes or fees unless the station's programs are popular. Independent sponsors, such as financial institutions or manufacturers, do not want their name associated with a failing station or individual program. Advertising agencies will not risk their clients' confidence by buying an unpopular slot. The clients themselves watch ratings very carefully before they part with money to promote their product or service. Popularity, therefore, is the most crucial factor in a station's profit margins.

National Stations

Every country regulates its broadcasting industry and provides a framework within which radio stations must work. This framework includes their finance structure, rules for granting licenses so that they can operate, and policies for allocating them **wavebands** (see also page 39).

Radio arrangements

The way radio is arranged depends a lot on how each nation itself is structured, in terms of how it is divided into metropolitan districts, counties, or states. It also depends on the political and economic systems and communications policies.

In some countries, in addition to national and local stations, there are also regional, state, and county stations. These stations reflect regional culture and broader interests and issues than those of local radio, and counteract the "capital-city" flavor of national stations. Regional radio is often publicly funded—an arm of national public radio, where that exists.

In Communist countries such as China, all forms of media are government controlled, even when it comes to content. In recent years, however, there has been a loosening of the tight rein held on radio by officials in these countries. In most other countries, government broadcasting regulations cover all stations, no matter how they are funded. Regulatory bodies can enforce policies by fining radio stations or removing their licenses. These bodies can control content to a certain extent as well. One of the most worrying issues for the Federal Communications Commission (FCC) is that commercial radio does not fulfill its public obligations—that is, to broadcast enough news, public health and weather warnings, and traffic and travel information and advice. Another issue is piracy—the copying of broadcast material. Concern about piracy has become more pressing with the development of Internet **digital** radio, which can be copied easily.

A voice for all

Most **democratic** nations try to encourage an independent voice in broadcasting. Even many tax-funded systems make sure of this by using the money to create a public broadcasting authority that is free of government control but still follows broadcasting guidelines. The Netherlands has developed a complex broadcasting system. It not only allows an independent voice, but also tries to take into account the country's diverse multicultural and multifaith society.

In the Netherlands, under the Media Act of 1988, two national organizations coordinate broadcasting—an independent group of businesses that provides production facilities, and a joint government and private sector company that **transmits** programs of general interest. The programs are produced by not-for-profit units that represent different interest groups—religious, artistic, and loosely political. Each group is funded through a tax paid by the nation's five million radio owners. The amount of money that each group receives depends on the number of its members.

Many small local stations represent minority interests and organizations, including unusual stations such as the Focus on the Family *radio theater, which broadcasts plays. This specialty transmission is known as* **narrowcasting** *and includes university and hospital radio stations, which are run on a shoestring, often with voluntary staff.*

In the United States

Ninety-nine percent of American households own a radio. Most stations are commercially funded through advertisements, but about ten percent are non-commercial, receiving contributions from corporations, individual sponsors, and government funding. The four original radio **networks**—the National Broadcasting Company (NBC), the Columbia Broadcasting System (CBS), the Mutual Broadcasting System, and the American Broadcasting Company (ABC)—are now owned by huge multinational corporations. By 1990, another big player, Rupert Murdoch, had added Fox Broadcasting to his newspaper and communications empire.

Who Is in Control?

The radio **producer** and **director** run individual radio programs. Unlike most television and film productions, the producer and director in radio are often the same person. In most radio stations, the producer and director cannot work alone. Nor do they take sole responsibility for the broadcast.

The scheme of things

There is great diversity in the way radio stations are managed. It all depends on the size of the station, the amount of money that is available, and the nature of the funding. In very small stations that are run on a shoestring budget, the owner, program planner, and producer are often the same person. The content of their output (what is **transmitted**) and hours of broadcasting are usually more limited.

The owner of a radio station has the ultimate responsibility for output and, to a certain extent, shapes its artistic and political content. The owners of national stations or **networks** are usually powerful multimedia people. They are rarely seen or heard, unlike owners of very small, independent local stations. A radio **station manager** is in charge of finances and makes sure that there is enough commercial sponsorship or public funding to sustain the right quantity and variety of programming. He or she is also responsible for what is broadcast from day to day. Program planners and producers set the schedule, working out which programs will fill the **slots** and determining the content. For commercial stations, they also allocate a certain amount of targeted advertising for each slot. The director for each program makes sure that each item is broadcast to the best effect and on time.

Interactive radio slots attract money as well as good ratings. Radio phone-in, fax, and e-mail discussions and contests allow people to participate. They are extremely popular and often generate large audiences.

Control, cash, and content

Program structuring, scheduling, and content are affected by methods and amounts of funding, **ratings,** trends, and ownership. Advertising, or the lack of it, is a crucial factor in program planning and content. Publicly financed programs are not usually broken up by commercials. Some listeners like the smooth, uninterrupted programming produced by public radio. Others find that it lacks sparkle. Advertisements can sometimes inject bursts of humor and music.

Ratings affect the type of show broadcast. To obtain higher ratings, research is conducted to work out the likely number and type of listeners at particular times of the day. These in turn affect the station's daily program schedule. Each program is targeted at a particular audience, based on age, income, ethnic origin, social background, and other factors. In the last twenty years, top-rated programs have been copied by producers of both local stations and national networks. This has led to a lack of variety, particularly among pop music stations. Commenting on the U.K.'s Sony Radio Awards (2000), U.K. journalist Anne Karpf stated, "Commercial radio, much of which is owned by a trio of large groups, is so **formatted** that innovation is a foreign word." The sameness is relieved only when a station is bold enough to try something new, but successful "novelties" are always copied, quickly making things stale again!

Radio road shows take music and chat around the country. Many pop radio stations also sponsor local or national concerts. Free tickets, invitations to talk to the presenters and musicians, and live acoustic "jam" sessions are all part of the package.

On the job

A station manager needs to know about finance in the media and have a good working knowledge of all aspects of radio production. He or she needs to have a good relationship with advertisers, radio producers, and presenters alike. Many station managers begin as producers for local radio, learning the type of advertisement or sponsorship needed for each slot.

In the Studio

Forget glamour—radio studios are usually small, claustrophobic, and totally lacking in luxury. This is especially true of local stations on a small budget. However, enthusiastic **directors,** presenters, and **audio technicians** can use the limited space and complex equipment to broadcast seamless shows.

Small is beautiful

Many local stations, particularly those used in colleges, hospitals, or other **narrowcast** organizations, **transmit** from a single room. While this means that production noise is difficult to get rid of, especially during a live show, modern technology is making it possible to produce a professional program in an ever-shrinking space. Even larger, national radio stations sometimes use single studios for a number of live programs, especially pop music shows.

Some programs, especially newscasts, use two rooms: a talk studio and a control room that is set behind a large window. Both of these rooms are soundproof. The talk studio allows for live, in-studio interviews and discussions among several people, rather than just phone-ins. There are several advantages to this. The discussion is more focused and is usually deeper as the participants talk face to face. The presenter has more control over the proceedings, and there is less chance of technical hiccups and poor sound quality, which phone-ins sometimes generate. The **producer**/director coordinates the program from the control room, while the **studio manager (SM)** handles the technical side—controlling **fades, cues,** and prerecorded material, such as the **signature tune** and prerecorded interviews.

*These long sliders on the mixing desk are called **faders**. Every sound channel that leads from a microphone has its own fader that is used to bring the sound in and then fade it up, down, or out. The SM uses the faders to balance sound, to end items, and to cue music, sound effects, and news items.*

The talk studio often consists only of a table, chairs, microphones, headphones, and sound channel leads wired into the control room. In the control room, sound from the microphones is balanced by the SM at the mixing desk. In a talk situation, many interviewees are inexperienced in microphone techniques—they sometimes speak too quietly, but more often, too loudly. The SM tries to compensate by decreasing the input from their microphone. There is not much that can be done about dead air, however, which is an often unexplainable silence caused by technical hitches.

Before the broadcast

Although early morning shows are live, there is a lot of preparation beforehand. For a new show, many prerecorded items have to be made or chosen, ranging from signature tunes and **jingles** to local commercials. Before the show goes on air, the producer and SM have to make sure that all the necessary equipment is in working order. Prerecorded tapes and CDs are put in playing order. Tape cartridges holding the jingles must be ready to plug in. The scripts for the day's news items are prepared on screen—most studios are now equipped with a computer monitor. Microphone levels are taken, and if more than one is being used, the SM makes sure that the sound coming through them is balanced. The presenter appears about 45 minutes before going on air to have another look at the schedule and the material.

The producer or director and the studio manager arrive in the studio before the presenter. There is a lot of equipment to be checked and set up, and a seamless show requires careful preparation beforehand.

Setting the Schedule

For our purposes, we will examine a local station operating as part of a commercial **network** that owns national as well as other local stations. This gives us an opportunity to take a look at a wide range of material and commercial issues surrounding a broad spectrum of **"drive-time"** shows.

The early bird . . .

The first thing the program planner needs to determine is the best time to run the program. A lot depends on the competition. **Prime time,** as we have seen, is about 6:30 to 9:30 A.M., but in many major cities more and more people are leaving for work early, as a large number commute from suburbs or rural areas. In response to this, many breakfast shows now begin at 6:00 A.M., when people are preparing for the day ahead. A station wishing to freshen its image with a new breakfast show might consider starting even earlier to catch the first listeners of the morning. From then on, it is a struggle with other stations to hold the listeners' attention with information and entertainment. A new breakfast show **format** might begin something like this:

5:45 Voice over faded-down catchy new **signature tune;** presenter of previous **slot** leads into the new breakfast show, introduces the recently-signed **freelance** presenter, tells everyone how wonderful he or she is, reminds listeners of the time, and signs off. (30 seconds)
Cue commercial for a major chain of coffeehouses. (30 seconds)

5:46 Cue brief news bulletin. (15 seconds)
Cue local weather update including airport, road, and railway conditions. (15 seconds)
Cue travel update including accidents, road construction, and reinforcing weather conditions affecting road, railway, and air travel. (15 seconds)
Fade in and up new signature tune again and fade down into presenter of new breakfast show who reminds listeners of the time, fades out the signature tune, introduces him or herself, and leads into a popular song. (15 seconds)

. . . Gets to work on time

In just two minutes the listeners know that something different is happening on the station. They are updated with news, weather, and travel, and they are reminded that they can break up their journey with a stop-off at a coffeehouse. They are also alerted to what time it is, a feature that continues throughout the prime-time show. This is a very important part of holding onto listeners who are in a hurry. As a safety issue, it also prevents drivers from continually looking at their clocks.

So far, the schedule is running exactly on time. But this show broadcasts pop music and local phone-in items as well as news and information. The length of tracks varies and interactive chats are unpredictable in length, so these tend to affect the schedule a little. News updates often do not occur exactly on the hour, or half-hour, but they are as near as possible. So, too, are commercial slots.

DJs have access to hundreds of CDs. Most well-known pop stations have a music policy set out by a **producer** or **director.** DJs can only play a few songs of their own choice.

On the job

A DJ, or disc jockey, needs a smooth voice with a good low note and the ability to keep talking in a calm, confident, but friendly manner. They also have to be quick thinkers to make interesting links between different slots in the program. A very good knowledge of commercial music and show business personalities is essential. Try working with a DJ at a school dance and start by taking a small slot in the program. Most DJs begin in voluntary radio, then progress to local radio. Some have acting qualifications.

Here, a local musician is playing live music on an early morning show. Guests have to be skillfully organized by the producer or director and the presenter so that they do not run too much over the scheduled time.

The Full Picture

Early morning shows are like eyes and ears for busy people. They try to give the listener a complete package of information—everything from a "recipe for today," to a suggestion for local evening entertainment. Occasionally their function is vital, providing medical and other advice, and even saving lives!

Not in the schedule

The portability and accessibility of radio make it one of the best ways of contacting people in an emergency situation. In times of crisis, local, national, and even international radio stations interrupt their schedule to make special calls to particular listeners asking them to contact their family or the police.

Sudden broadcasts are sometimes made on a much larger scale, alerting people to life-threatening emergency situations. In countries where there are many kinds of natural disasters, radio stations are linked to disaster warning systems. The U.S. and Japan in particular have developed close links with radio, particularly in their earthquake, hurricane, tornado, and tsunami (tidal wave) zones. The U.S. also uses radio as part of its flood warning system. Instruments such as flood meters and earthquake seismometers trigger warning systems at local stations.

Vital links

The National Weather Center has permanently open emergency links with both television and radio stations that interrupt their regular schedule when different levels of alert need to be broadcast. In Tornado Alley, a vast tract of southern and central states, professional "twister chasers" alert local weather centers and radio stations when tornado-bearing clouds begin to look dangerous. Radio warnings enable people living and working in the twister's path to seek safety in tornado shelters, while motorists have a chance to get out of their cars—one of the most dangerous places to be during a tornado. Radio also plays an important part in smooth evacuation. It is rare, however, for the final tornado warning to occur in the middle of an early morning show; most twisters strike in the late afternoon and early evening, just as people are leaving their offices and factories. The **prime-time** breakfast show can be used to inform listeners that suspicious-looking clouds are on the way.

The final fade

Before the final **fade,** a prime-time show often leads the listener into the next program with a **trail**—a short section of the item if it is prerecorded, such as a play, or a descriptive introduction if it is live. The presenter will try to set the listener up for the rest of the day, ending on a cheerful note and reminding the listener of the evening's entertainment, not only on the radio station but also on television, at the movies, the theater, or on choice websites.

Later in the day, the liveliest or most controversial moments of a prime-time breakfast show are rebroadcast, reminding loyal listeners what they will miss if they don't tune in the next day. These trailers are also designed to encourage new listeners to switch from their regular station to a new one in those vital early-morning hours.

*Countries with poor road, rail, and air communications rely heavily on radio in emergency situations. In a disaster situation, like the floods seen here in Somalia, **two-way radio** is often used to coordinate rescue teams and the distribution of emergency supplies. Local radio keeps dispersed, trapped, and isolated people informed about the disaster and the relief effort.*

Technical tips

Once an emergency warning has been broadcast, the presenter needs to bring the listener back into the program with a snappy introduction or perhaps a **jingle.** Jingles and special effects are used especially on morning pop and "zoo" shows to "glue" items together as links and leads or break them up to jolt the listener. Effects can be prerecorded inside or outside the studio and faded in from tapes. Noises like gushing water and echoes can also be held **digitally** and accessed by computer. Voice echo can be achieved by the "echo mike" or synthesizer.

All in a Day's Work

Breaking the News

Producing news items throughout the day is a bit of a juggling act and involves covering the main headlines of the morning while also including breaking news stories as they occur. Some features, particularly updates of the world's money markets, are staple breakfast-news items, but by the early evening, many of the morning's headlines might only get brief mentions as the day's "other stories." In times of crisis, however, or during events such as elections, the headlines remain the same for several days as do the topics for talk shows that follow.

The person listening to the local radio show expects to be familiar with the places and people they are hearing about. It is this familiarity that keeps a local audience tuned in and makes them feel like a part of the community, even if they have to leave it for the greater part of the day.

Sniffing out the story

"Headlines" and "stories" are words taken from another news medium—the newspaper. Radio is not very different in its methods of collecting news items. Radio journalists are often **freelance** general journalists, also employed by newspapers and other media.

Radio takes advantage of on-the-spot coverage of events around the world, such as demonstrations, disasters, sports events, political rallies, ceremonies, and elections. A good sports commentator enables the listener to visualize a game through detailed description and lively presentation. This requires a lot of knowledge, especially for diverse sports carried out at world events such as the Olympic Games.

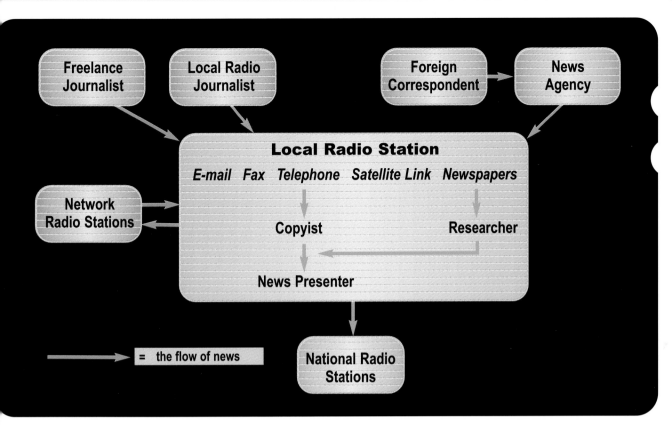

This diagram shows how news flows into a local radio station. Some of the news also flows out again to national radio stations, which rely on local networks to supply information on events occurring in remote parts of the country.

Many news items come second-hand, via other media, or they are **network** items from other radio stations, some of which are prerecorded overnight. Pop stations often present only brief bulletins with the occasional opinion thrown in by the DJ and listeners. They very rarely contain original material researched by their own journalists. To keep up-to-date with its stories, a radio station sometimes uses established news agencies, such as the Associated Press and United Press International, or Reuters in the U.K. and Agence France-Presse in France.

Sending the story

For radio, all these stories are either sent to the station by e-mail or fax, or phoned in and taken down by a person called a copyist. With mobile phone and hand-held satellite communication systems, radio has become an immediate source of the latest information. Network radio stations can now share stories through computer systems interconnected by telephone lines. Live reporters have a limited time to give a rounded view of a situation—sometimes a mere phone call's-worth of facts, opinions, and interviews. **Prime-time** radio listeners often tune in only to catch up with the main headlines and very basic issues surrounding them.

On the job

A radio journalist needs good research and writing skills and the ability to construct clear, concise reports suitable for the radio medium. He or she has to be able to communicate well with the public and people in high places alike. You could begin by writing news bulletins for your school newspaper and reading broadcasts for your local hospital or college radio. Make sure you tape any of your work that is broadcast. It can be used to build a portfolio to present at an interview.

Let's Take a Commercial Break

Most **prime-time** shows are funded by sponsors and commercials, both local and national. The bulk of the commercials pay for the capital costs of a station and its permanent staff, as well as for music **royalties** (payment paid to a band when its song is played). Special **slots,** such as contests, advice sessions, and phone-ins are often sponsored separately by businesses.

How does radio advertise itself? Sometimes you will see T-shirts, bumper stickers, and billboards promoting a particular station. Now there are also radio advertisements on the Internet. Most of the advertising is carried out by presenters reminding you of whom you are listening to and what **waveband** *you are tuned into.*

What is being offered?

Commercials are spoken advertisements. (The term "advertisement" usually refers to written ads, still images used in newspapers and magazines, or ads on billboards.) Radio commercials range from **jingles** and **voice-overs** lasting just a few seconds to half-minute and minute-long slots. These longer commercials are often dramatized.

Radio commercials advertise not only manufactured products and financial services, but also charities and public initiatives, such as anti-drunk-driving campaigns. Other types of information include reminders to pay taxes on time and to watch or listen to political broadcasts. Government-funded commercials like these are usually aired on both public and private radio stations. They are the only kind of commercial that many publicly-owned stations are allowed to run.

Election issues

Usually, professional newscasters around the world do not give an opinion on a party political issue when an election is due to occur. This includes local elections and referenda, like the 1999 Australian referendum on severing ties with the British monarchy, where each person in the country could vote yes or no. There are many political talk shows in the U.S., however, where opinions are given freely. As we shall see on page 40, there are other restrictions placed on radio advertising.

The right slot

We have seen that the first commercial for the new breakfast show on Monday morning advertised a chain of coffeehouses—a good time to plug their product. Finding suitable slots during the day or night and the right time of year is important. No one, for instance, wants to hear a commercial for central heating during a heat wave!

Unfortunately, however, the timing of commercials is not always under the program scheduler's complete control. Prime-time radio can especially command high fees for its commercial slots, and an inappropriate product might simply be the one that can pay the most money. However, it is not in the interest of a product manufacturer, service provider, or radio station to allow poor timing to make their advertising ineffective. Internet radio has no need to break for advertisements— banner ads flash constantly at the side or top of the web page.

Making the most of it

National holidays, such as Thanksgiving, are exploited by radio presenters, product manufacturers, and advertisers alike. So, too, are celebrations such as Christmas, Easter, and Mother's Day. Saint Patrick's Day is also a target for commercials. In 2000, a product promoted for Saint Patrick's Day was re-advertised for a fictional "Saint Terry's Day" on the following Friday! This exploited the high profile of Saint Patrick's Day, extending the commercial's life-span very quickly and cheaply for another week.

Luring the Listener

Radio commercials have to work very hard to attract listeners. The writing and acting have to compensate for the lack of visual images. Among the huge range of styles and production techniques, it is often the element of surprise that makes people sit up and listen.

Simple or slick?

Local commercials are produced cheaply and often consist of short **jingles** with a simple **voice-over.** In small, local radio stations, the voice-over may be performed live by the presenter or the DJ rather than prerecorded by a separate announcer. These are usually not the most imaginative of commercials, but they do nudge people into exploring local facilities.

National or **network** stations broadcast more commercials for well-known brands and labels. The commercials can be very slick or even very bizarre, but in either case they cost more money to record. Actors perform small sketches—even miniature sitcoms that change every few weeks. Opposite is an imaginary script for a commercial. Try to guess what it is advertising before you reach the end. You can read more about performing for radio on pages 28 and 30.

*Jingles are recorded to advertise not only goods and services, but also the radio station's own **slots** and presenters. Short jingles with singing often get a message across more effectively than longer, more complex spoken advertisements, which require the listener to concentrate harder and longer.*

How do they do it?

The following fictitious commercial is technically quite simple, with spoken words, few sound effects, and no distracting background music or jingles. The commercial captures the listener's attention with its humor and by keeping the audience guessing as to what product is being advertised. This is how you would generally expect to see a radio commercial script—known as copy—set out, with instructions for the actor underlined and in square brackets. Instructions for the control room are written in capital letters. The content of this commercial, as with all others, would be regulated by the Federal Communications Commission (FCC).

FADE IN AND UP

ACTOR: [Dreamy, romantic, and tortured, tapping frantically at a keyboard]
Anna, oh Anna, wrenching my heart like an adjustable wrench.
Er—wrench? . . . Maybe not.
[Sighs, deletes text, and starts again]
Your eyes gleam and glisten— stars in the sky,
Moist and brown like a wet mud pie . . .
[Frustrated angst]
No, NO—it just won't DO!
[Creative, tortured voice]
I am mesmerized by your magnetic face
Because you look like something from outer . . .
(and here the listener is supposed to complete the rhyme with "space!")
[Frustrated rage]
Help me, Shakespeare, I just can't do it!
FADE TO BLACK

*Jingles and advertisements are **cued** by a DJ, using equipment such as a computer, or the cart machine (center) and **faders** seen here.*

After the "poet's" agonizing, a bright but sensible voice tells him he would be better off taking his loved one out for a candle-lit dinner than trying to write a love poem. So have we finally gotten to the the point of the commercial? No, not yet! It is not promoting a restaurant. Only at the end do we know the key product being advertised—a limousine service company specializing in luxury vehicles for that special journey. The name of the company is then repeated by the calm voice-over to reinforce the brand's name in our minds.

Easy Listening

It may all sound easy, but presenting and announcing on radio requires a great amount of skill. With live radio, the presenter always has to be prepared to react to the unexpected—a surprising news story, an irate listener, or even a blown fuse. More than this, the presenter's voice must keep the audience tuned in.

It's all in the voice

Local radio lacks the resources for a large group of presenters and **continuity** announcers. It relies on the vocal skills of a limited number of people to keep the listener interested. While clarity must be maintained, presenters must also vary their **pitch** and tone, or **intonation pattern.** Presenters seem to talk naturally, especially on informal breakfast shows, but they are acutely aware of their vocal patterns. A presenter must not allow the tone of his or her voice to be flat, the pace of his or her speech to be repetitive, or the ends of his or her sentences to **fade.**

It is easy to tell that presenters and announcers work hard at their voice production when they are compared with inexperienced listeners on phone-ins. The caller's intonation is usually even, and the pitch quite high. This is less compelling than the voice of a professional presenter or announcer.

Pitch										
high										
medium										
low										
	I	can't	be-lieve	I'm	on	the	ra-dio	—	I'm	so	exci-ted!

high										
medium										
low										
	I	can't	be-lieve	I'm	on	the	ra-dio	—	I'm	so	exci-ted!

Try reading these sentences aloud to a friend, following the rising and falling intonation patterns shown, but using the same noise level for each. You will probably find that one pattern seems more interesting, and the other more boring.

While varying intonation keeps people tuned in, research shows that there are certain voice pitch levels and particular intonation patterns that are more attractive than others. A normally low pitch level is apparently more attractive than a high one. Spoken English has a restricted set of intonation patterns, but it seems that alternating between a rising and falling ending keeps us all listening, and a presenter with a wide tonal range is more interesting than one with a narrow spectrum. In recent years there has been a trend for some reporters and presenters to end their sentences on a stressed high syllable. This type of intonation is known as "upspeak." For a time it was quite popular, but some feel it has become overused and irritating.

No second chance

For commercials, prerecording allows an announcer or actor to do several **takes,** which gives him or her a chance to achieve the required voice control, pitch, intonation pattern, and expression. Live presenters and continuity announcers have no such luxury and instead develop a set number of intonation patterns and pitch levels, which they use for most situations. These have to be continually reevaluated by the **producer,** who wants to avoid monotony. Only after a program can these things be properly ironed out. Presenters must also keep the sound going and keep the listener glued to the station; there is never a good time to pause. This is called continuity and is a much sought-after skill among radio presenters.

Many breakfast shows have more than one presenter. It is important that they have an easy relationship with each other and can improvise at will. Presenters are often chosen for their contrasting characters, but it is equally important that their voice quality and intonation not be too similar.

Clear delivery

Radio has affected the way we judge spoken language and has influenced the way it is taught in our schools. Received Pronunciation (RP), or standard pronunciation, developed from early radio presenters' delivery and was marked by its clarity and lack of a strong regional accent. This style was copied by many educators.

Acting for Advertisements

Acting for radio commercials is the same as for radio drama, except that it is very concentrated. In any type of radio acting, every word and change of the voice counts, and every tiny sound that you make is heard.

Hearing is believing

The radio actor has to get into character in the same way as for any other medium. Many actors "feel" each part they play using a technique known as method acting. The first step in method acting is to study every aspect of the role, to "live" it. This means the actors must first rid themselves of much of their own identity.

Radio commercials are so short that there is little time to get into character. The experienced **voice-over** actor develops a technique using short bursts of deep concentration to block out everything else and acquires a knack for knowing quickly what the advertiser is trying to achieve. It is similar to having a short bit-part in a film, except that in the case of commercials, the actor often has to take the listener through an entire miniature plot rather than portray the character amid a much larger scenario.

Being natural

An actor has to make up for the fact that the listener cannot see facial expressions or body gestures, so he or she has to find action and reaction through the voice. This does not mean overacting—in fact, it takes a lot of conscious thought and control to seem normal without appearing dull. The sound of an average person on the street is often exactly what advertising companies want. In a radio play, if everything sounds highly dramatic there is no contrast—the words and the plot lose their impact and meaning. Many **directors** for commercials play it safe by employing an actor with what is called a "brown" voice, which is a steady, older, male voice with friendly, confident low tones.

Studio time

It takes a whole day in the studio to rehearse and record just half an hour of a radio play. But a one-minute commercial voice-over takes comparatively little time; often just a few minutes, even with several **takes.** Studio time is expensive, so every commercial will be given a production **slot** and a tight schedule to work with. Some directors even use a stopwatch. The actor usually sees the script just a few minutes before recording, so there is no time to rehearse. The schedule also has to allow for preproduction time spent in setting up the studio and testing the equipment.

Working from home

Regular commercial actors have studios set up in their own homes. They link with the studio control room directly through special phone lines (called Integrated Services Digital Network, or ISDN), or they make prerecorded tapes that are then mixed with sound effects and **jingles** in the postproduction stage.

Radio commercial voice-overs are often recorded in sound booths. Actors can be given several scripts to reel off in just one session.

On the job

A radio actor needs a broad voice range with a strong low note, sensitivity to sound, and a lot of patience! Try studying first for stage or screen acting and then get experience as an announcer on a local college or hospital radio station. Finally, make a demonstration tape to send to studios and production companies. Begin with your own voice explaining who you are. Then record a few 30-second slot scripts for real products in a range of voices, none of them being too extreme.

The Big Stage

More complex radio commercials that involve several actors are performed in a studio using several microphones. This is more like a radio play, which requires a lengthy and more technically complex process, using sound effects and movement.

Doors, drawers, cupboards, and curtains are often set on wheels so that they can be opened or closed at the right microphone. Here, a special effects technician is opening and closing a door. Sound effects like these are sometimes done by the actors themselves.

Moving around the mikes

In the studio, the red light is on—that is the **cue** for the first **take.** Each of the actors has his or her own cue light and speaks through a numbered microphone. On the script, the microphones are numbered too, with every character's lines. This shows the actors where they should position themselves. Sometimes they have to move silently from one microphone to another. At other times the underlined instructions on the script indicate that the actors' movements around the studio should be audible.

Directors usually like to rehearse and then record a scene in one particular sound set, using effects like those you can see in the picture on page 32. Then they move on to a different sound set, not necessarily in the order of the plot. This method is known as rehearse-record. Occasionally, directors like to rehearse the whole performance and then record it in sequence. This is called recording at-a-run.

Making a noise

If you have ever been to a pop concert, you may have noticed that when performers speak into the mike between songs, they do not always get the smooth, crisp sound that they achieve when they are singing and playing instruments. Usually, this is because they speak too loudly right on top of the microphone, causing popping and blasting. Popping is the fluffy, fizzy sound of explosive consonants—these are the letters b, p, t, d, k, and hard c. Blasting is the distortion of the sound.

You can hear for yourself how easy it is to "pop." Put your mouth close to the rim of a long drinking glass or the neck of a glass bottle and voice the explosive consonants over it. Then repeat the letters, but with your mouth about an inch or two away from the rim of the glass. You will notice that the second time the consonants sound clearer and less resonant (booming).

When actors make a mistake the director calls for another take, which is edited into the complete scene at the postproduction stage. For commercials, monologues (plays performed by just one actor), and book readings, the editor often asks for the tape to be rewound to a spot just before the fault. The actor then listens to the **pitch** and tempo of the piece and continues, correcting the previous mistake.

The editor is responsible for making sure that all the different takes are fitted together to produce a smooth finished item. Editors often have to shorten prerecorded items by removing unwanted sounds or words to ensure that they fit the required time **slot.**

Setting the scene

The live acting studio is equipped with hard screens to create live or bright sound and soft, cloth-covered screens for dead sound. For a damped-down, outdoor effect the studio walls are padded. Different surfaces on the floor and a set of stairs provide realistic sound effects as the actor or **studio manager** moves. The surfaces can include carpet, wood, concrete, and stone. Actors and special effects technicians sometimes have to dress in costume, especially in a period play. This is so that the materials rustle and flap with an authentic sound. Technicians also engage in fight scenes and perform other sounds, such as turning on water faucets.

Making mistakes

These are some of the problems faced by radio performers:

✿ Crashing in—not allowing the previous actor to finish his or her lines. Some actors try too hard to bite the cue (come in on their cue in good time).
✿ Going into the dead—moving out of a mono mike's field of sound.
✿ Pitching up—copying the pitch level of a fellow actor's voice.
✿ Rustling the script and tapping or blowing into the mike—a director's nightmare!
✿ Fluffing words—the simple problem of not forming words properly.

Turn on the Radio

How Does It Sound?

Sound waves are completely invisible. So how can we identify and control them, and how are they transferred from their source to an audience? Understanding how sound works is crucial not only to a radio station's technical experts, but also to its **directors,** presenters, and actors.

The ways of radio waves

Radio sound is communicated through equipment that changes sound into electromagnetic waves, which travel in straight lines through space. Electromagnetic waves are vibrating electric and magnetic fields of force that radiate from their source. There are different bands of waves with different functions (radio, infrared, visible light, etc.). These waves are all part of the electromagnetic range, or spectrum. Radio waves can travel very long distances by means of **transmitters.** The waves are picked up by the **receiver** in your radio set, which converts the electromagnetic waves back into sound. This process describes **analog** broadcasting.

Tuning in

Every radio station **transmits** on its own **frequency,** like a railway track for sound waves. Different types of radio stations use different frequencies, and it is very important for a station to be available on the frequency of its choice. Of course, nothing will be heard without a radio receiver. High-quality radio sound needs a sensitive receiver to pick up the frequency.

The radio's **fidelity** should be high, which means that the receiver should respond so that all audio frequencies are amplified, or made stronger, equally. The ability to receive radio signals from one station and reject those from another on a nearby frequency is important as well. A good radio also filters out or shields unwanted noise, such as hums, whistles, or hisses.

Sounds different

Sound is heavily manipulated inside the studio. The way in which the voice is expressed and effects are made, the way microphones are used, and the nature of the space in which sound is created all affect the resulting broadcast. This does not only refer to the volume of the sound, but also the quality—whether it is clear or muffled, resonant (booming) or dead. Such differences are used to create a particular atmosphere or bring contrast to the program. They also reveal to the listener the environment a sound is supposed to be coming from—maybe outside on a windy cliff, or inside an echoing cathedral. News reporters really do broadcast live news items from such places. However, if, for instance, a drama or advertisement requires the characteristics of these sound environments, they can be created very realistically, and more reliably, inside the studio, as we saw on page 32.

The first radio

Who invented radio? In the late nineteenth century, many scientists from Europe and the U.S. contributed to our knowledge of radio waves and electronics—the two fields of study needed to create radio as we know it today. Many people attribute the invention of radio to the Italian electrical engineer Guglielmo Marconi, who, by 1899, had established commercial communication between the U.K. and France. By 1902, the first crackly radio links crossed the Atlantic from the U.K. to the U.S.

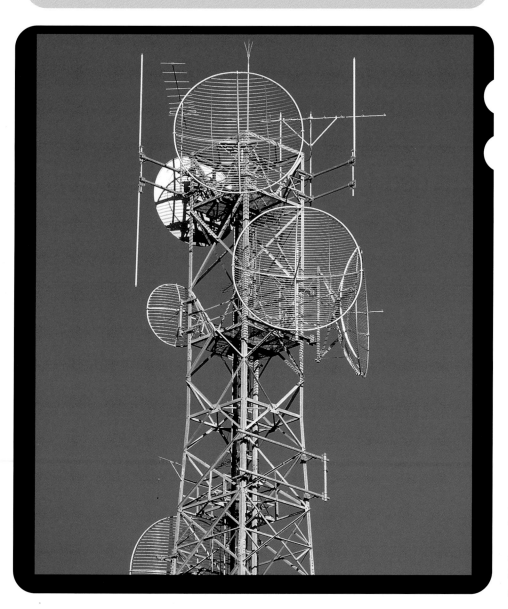

Radio transmission towers are often very tall and vulnerable to bad weather. Many people also object to these towers being located near their homes.

On the job

If you want to work as a sound engineer in a radio station, you will need to study science and mathematics at school. You then need a good grasp of electronics, sound systems, and, increasingly, information technology. These can be combined in a sound engineer's course. Try working as a volunteer at a local radio station to get studio experience.

Catching the Waves

Thousands of listeners have turned on their radios and tuned into the early morning show on the regular **waveband,** and the station is still there as usual. How does the program reach its audience? And what do the letters and numbers on radio sets mean?

Looking at your radio

Your radio set is a **receiver.** Basically, it reverses the process of the **transmitter** by changing electric impulses back into sound. When you turn on your radio set, you are linking it to a transmitter, often miles away. The transmitter in turn links to the radio station. Each of these three pieces of equipment uses **antennae** or aerials to catch the **frequency** of radio waves that carry the program. Your radio has to be tuned so that it will receive the correct frequency. But what are frequencies, and what are waves?

Radio waves, like light waves, have different lengths and speeds. They are used for different types of transmission—for radio, telephones, television, radar, navigational systems, and space communication. Each kind of wave travels with a kind of pulse, or frequency, moving at a certain number of cycles every second. The shortest waves have the most cycles per second, or the highest frequency. The longest waves have the least cycles per second, or the lowest frequency.

The cycles per second are known as hertz and are named after the early German radio scientist, Heinrich Hertz. If you look on your radio, you might see markings such as MHz and kHz. These abbreviations represent two of the different cycle speeds: kHz stands for kilohertz, which run at a rate of 1,000 cycles per second, and MHz stands for megahertz, which represents one million cycles per second. So, kHz have a lower frequency than MHz.

The ionosphere is a band of gas layers wrapped around the earth's upper atmosphere. Short wavelengths can penetrate the ionosphere to reach satellite stations. From the stations, information can be transmitted all over the world. However, the ionosphere prevents long wavelengths from reaching space, making them bounce back down to earth. This is why long wavelengths are only used to transmit information within a small area.

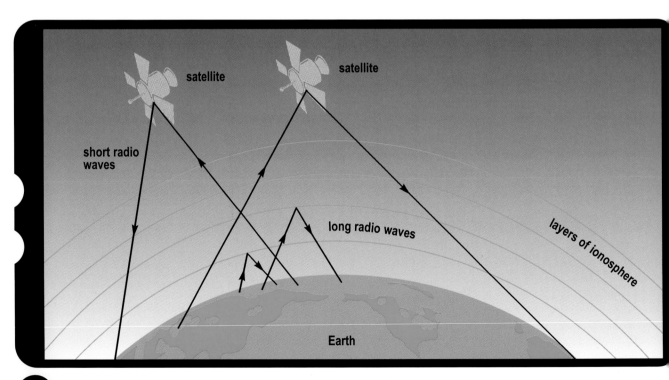

*Both terrestrial **analog** radio and cable are difficult to receive in mountainous terrain. Apart from the mountains themselves interfering with signals, it is often too difficult to set up transmitters or lay cable. The future will likely bring more broadcasting via satellite.*

A good reception

Sound waves sent from a radio station to your set are **transmitted** on **carrier waves.** These are continuous electrical oscillations (vibrations) generated by transmitters. But in order to receive all the different types of sound, carrier waves have to be modulated (varied). AM and FM are two types of modulated carrier wave. AM stands for Amplitude **Modulation,** which indicates that the strength of the wave is varied in order to accept different sounds. FM stands for Frequency Modulation, which means that the frequency of the wave is varied.

An increasing number of stations are broadcasting on the much-favored FM, which is more varied and also more stable than AM. AM tends to pick up more static **interference** from activity such as the lightning storm in the picture on page 38. FM is able to reproduce different kinds of sound more faithfully than AM because its frequency range is much greater. FM, however, is usually carried on very high frequencies and very short waves, which means it does not travel as far as AM, which is often carried on low frequencies and longer waves. To compensate, the transmitting antennae for FM stations often have to be very tall in order for the signal to go as far as possible. As placing tall antennae is often very impractical, FM stations are successfully broadcast through telephone wires or special cable, such as those used for cable TV.

Hearing Clearly

There are a limited number of **carrier waves** in the electromagnetic spectrum (see page 34), so only a limited number of stations can **transmit** programs within a certain geographic area. How does radio manage to reach most people clearly, without **interference?**

*Radio waves can be disrupted or distorted by electrical interference, or static. Electrical storms and electrical equipment, such as **two-way radios**, car ignition systems, and high-powered sewing machines that have not been properly shielded, all affect radio waves. The circuits of radios themselves should be properly shielded from external interference by a highly conductive or magnetic material.*

Technical tips

Cellular radio is a transmission system designed to make radio signals clearer and more available. It consists of a **network** of hexagonally arranged waveband "cells," each having their own **transmitter**. As you travel, your **receiver** automatically tunes into each cell, or transmitter, in turn. Cell-phones and other personal communication systems, such as pagers and voice mail, use this radio network.

Sharing the waves

The potential problem of interference has led each nation to control how many stations can operate and who gets what **waveband.** Of course, a government cannot legislate for other countries, which is why you can sometimes hear interference from a station belonging to a bordering country. Most countries control broadcasting through a department of communications. This department ensures that wavebands are fairly and effectively distributed, and that a code of conduct is administered that all radio stations must abide by. This practical governmental role in allocating wavebands has inevitably led to governments also being responsible for regulating the industry in terms of program content and station broadcasting rights.

A rigid control of wavebands ensures that reception is clear for all radio stations. In countries such as the U.S., where there are thousands of radio stations, it is very important to stay strictly within the bandwidth limit. A deviation of just one hundredth of one percent causes serious interference with even distant stations on the same **frequency.**

A larger audience

Most local and national radio stations hope to be granted FM waves wherever their programs are transmitted. The number of BBC World Service listeners rose from 143 million in 1999 to 151 million in 2000. The increase is attributed to the station changing some of its transmission from AM to local FM, which has made reception clearer and available to a wider audience. It is now also broadcast on the Internet.

The radio microphone carried by this presenter has its own transmitter fitted inside a small box and worn around the waist. The radio transmitter enables the presenter to walk around freely without being restricted by cable.

Useful radio

Radio has enabled some instruments to operate more precisely, conveniently, or efficiently. The radio compass uses radio waves to find directions. The radio pill is a miniature radio transmitter enclosed in a tiny capsule. When swallowed, it sends out information about what is going on inside the body. Radio telescopes give us an idea of the shape of objects in space by picking up radio waves emitted from them.

You Can't Say That!

The early morning show is a seamless concoction of music, news, and talk, but are all the listeners happy about what they hear? It is difficult for a show packed with opinion not to offend at least one listener. What happens when it does?

Is it right? Is it fair?

Broadcasting authorities throughout the world regulate most aspects of radio transmission. These regulations range from the number of stations that any one company can own and the proportion of commercials that can be **transmitted,** to the extent to which owners of stations and journalists can air their own views. Most countries also enforce policies and create laws concerning fairness, equality, decency, taste, swearing, sex, and violence. These policies try to ensure that listeners are not offended by anything that they hear, and that young people will be protected from themes that are too adult in content.

Each station is responsible for complying with these laws and usually has specialist media and **libel** lawyers at hand if a program is in danger of making statements that hover on the edge of legality. Breaking the regulations can mean a fine or even the removal of the station's license. Broadcasting regulations, however, may sometimes conflict with laws ensuring freedom of speech.

Listeners keep radio stations alive, and it is against the interests of a station not to respond to their complaints. Sometimes, however, a station has to choose between keeping listeners who tune in specifically for the sensationalism, or keeping those who object to it.

Making a complaint

What happens if listeners hear something on the radio that they find offensive? How do they complain? The first course of action is to contact the radio station. Most stations broadcast a **slot** that allows listeners to express their opinion concerning the programs, either in writing or through a phone-in. Large stations also have a complaints unit that will answer queries individually. Aside from that, listeners can contact the Federal Communications Commission (FCC) or separate radio authority. Some countries operate different complaints authorities for publicly financed and commercial broadcasting. There is also sometimes a separate organization for monitoring advertising standards, ensuring that their guidelines have not been breached. Media magazines usually carry the names and addresses of these agencies, as well as the week's program listings.

One form of free speech not allowed in most countries is that of using someone's name or voice for personal gain. In radio this applies particularly to impersonations in commercials, which is why it is essential for all actors and presenters to develop their own voice and style.

*Heated political debate before elections is good for both politicians and **ratings,** and radio has a long political history in the United States. During the 1930s and '40s, President Franklin Roosevelt made regular broadcasts to the nation outlining his policies. These "fireside chats" and his calm, friendly tone increased his popularity.*

Radio rights

The Federal Communications Commission (FCC) is responsible for regulating broadcasting. This includes the granting and revocation of licenses, as well as the allocation of **wavebands.** It also ensures that the content and presentation of programs conform to laws. Until 1987, stations were required to comply with the Fairness Doctrine, which denied the right of station proprietors to express their own political and social views. And until the 1990s, the FCC also restricted the growth of cable stations. After this time, many restraints were lifted and the broadcasting industry was deregulated, allowing more freedom and competition for all media stations.

The Verdict

So what do listeners think of their early morning radio show? How does the rest of the media respond to it? Through reviews and **ratings,** the **producer** and the owner of a station learn whether they have the right formula.

What did they think?

"The audience is the final factor" is a common saying in the media and entertainment world. In radio, it refers to the fact that the response of the public is an interaction—a way of participating in a show and of shaping its future—for in turn, radio stations will react to the public's response. Some of the most pressing issues are knowing what to change, when to change it, or even if change is necessary at all. It is easy for listeners to find a station that keeps up with the times better than their regular station, or a station that has not changed so much that it has lost its original appeal.

Market researchers ask about a listener's age group, social and economic bracket, and general tastes, as well as his or her listening habits. This information gives them an idea of the profile of their average listener. Radio stations cannot afford to upset their listener base, but at the same time, they need to know if that base is changing and why.

Finding out what listeners think of the program is crucial for both the station and advertisers. Both conduct surveys using telephone questionnaires and focus groups, among other techniques. They also take very careful consideration of any points raised in phone-ins and letters.

Local radio stations and advertisers can take samplings by locating listeners via local telephone directories and electoral registries. Local radio **networks** combine the results to find out what programs work best in certain regions. National radio, with its vast resources, can use a wider range of sampling techniques or employ ratings companies to assess the success or failure of stations, presenters, particular programs, or even small **slots** within them. In the U.S., the larger media companies use well-established organizations, such as Nielsen Ratings. Internet radio listeners might find their listening habits silently monitored by agencies using **digital** technology to find out their tastes, and therefore the kinds of advertisements they can direct toward them. There are serious privacy issues concerning these techniques.

Very public opinion

Last, but by no means least, what did the reviewers think? A new local radio show can expect to receive a comment in the media column of the local newspaper, but a national radio station breakfast show will find reviews in national newspapers and media magazines. These same publications, both local and national, will also be represented at the major award ceremonies for radio **producers, directors,** and presenters, as will manufacturers of radio **receivers** and other radio equipment. Otherwise, radio prizes are usually tucked behind more prestigious media at what are really newspaper, television, and film award ceremonies, unless they are rewarded in the U.S., where the prestigious annual Silver Microphone Awards acknowledge program makers and advertising agencies working only in local and state radio. The categories range from "best use of humor" in an advertisement to the "best broadcast non-English program" for ethnic minority listeners.

Radio award ceremonies have been criticized for giving out prizes to the same presenters and production teams again and again. The names of presenters in particular, and especially DJs, crop up regularly as winners. This should not be a surprise; many well-known radio personalities stay in the business for several decades, their charisma earning good ratings for the radio stations they work for. The elite, especially those working on **prime-time** breakfast shows, work very hard at keeping their voice fresh without losing their original attraction. It is this balance of trying to lure new listeners, and yet not lose all of the old ones, that keeps presenters, producers, and **station managers** permanently on their toes.

Garrison Keillor

What, and who, lasts in radio? If Garrison Keillor is anything to go by, a live show with a mish-mash of comedy sketches, acoustic music from guest artists, and the gentle stories of his mythical Lake Wobegone folk are a winning formula. He has written and presented the *Prairie Home Companion* show for about 24 years now. Radio continues to produce a core of high-profile writers, presenters, and DJs. Their legacy often lies in the catchphrases they have coined, which linger on in our language.

The Future

No one knows how **prime-time** radio will develop. Its trends will doubtless run parallel to the ever-changing needs of busy people the world over. Radio's future also rests on its making use of technological advances in the **digital** age.

Radio for all

The continuation of nationally controlled and financed radio stations enables the majority of people world-wide to have easy access to information and entertainment. Satellite communications have also allowed the numbers of small stations and amateur radio to grow, ensuring that minority interests are well served and that radio stays alive and accessible to all. Since the 1960s, radio satellites, known as OSCARs (Orbiting Satellites Carrying Amateur Radio), have opened up the waves to amateur **transmissions.** These transmissions have ridden "piggyback" on major communication satellites for nearly 40 years, but it is the Internet that has transformed radio since the mid-1990s.

Internet radio shows have become increasingly popular and, in time, will probably lead to the creation of an international breakfast show **format.** The Internet is being used more and more for interactive radio shows and their website spin-offs, expanding the function of radio with on-line gimmicks such as quizzes and contests. On-line presenters can now integrate an almost infinite amount of Internet information into their shows. With no need for commercial breaks, over 90 percent of an Internet radio show can be dedicated to music or chat.

Eliot Stein is already beginning to influence breakfast shows with his softer style. In 2000, the U.K.'s prestigious BBC Radio One pop music breakfast show formally dropped the "zoo" format and began to include more serious news items.

Eliot Stein is the pioneer of the on-line talk show, which he introduced in 1994. In the early days, you had to log into the chat because the program was in text only. In 1996, Stein launched the first live audible show, creating a forum for topical discussion. Unlike the "zoo" formula described on page 7, his **slots** are non-confrontational, allowing information-sharing rather than trying to increase **ratings** with public show-downs and pranks.

Ordinary mobile phones now have Internet links for radio phone-in items and portable on-line sets with screens. WAP (Wireless Application Protocol) technology is exclusive, however, and is really only available to rich nations or the few wealthy members of poorer ones, and it is a luxury for people in some countries, where Internet access is quite expensive.

Free radio?

Millions of people around the world do not have access to a reliable source of electricity or money for batteries. The whole of humankind faces the possibility of dwindling energy resources and the ever-increasing problem of battery disposal. Inventions such as the wind-up radio (see also page 8) provide practical technology for a more environmentally friendly future.

This wind-up radio has a clockwork mechanism inside that generates and stores enough electricity for about one hour of listening after a 30-second windup. Similar, solar-powered radios are also available.

Technical tips

✡ One of the latest broadcasting techniques involves converting radio waves into a computerized form known as digital transmission. It is easier to control and manipulate than **analog** (see page 34), and digital transmission can be broadcast on very high frequencies (see page 37). It also takes up less transmission space than analog.

✡ An analog-to-digital (A/D) converter is an integrated circuit (a microchip) that allows a digital computer to accept data from an analog device. The A/D converter is also called a digitizer. Sound in digital form is more stable than its analog counterpart.

Glossary

air time the time allowed for a particular broadcast to take place, whether it is a program, commercial, or another slot

analog sound that is translated into radio waves by a radio station's transmitter and then translated back to sound inside the listener's radio set

antenna (or aerial) a structure for sending out and receiving sound signals

audio technician person who makes sure that sound equipment in a radio station works properly

carrier wave wave generated by a transmitter to carry the sound waves sent out by a radio station

continuity to be without breaks or pauses. A radio announcer who links programs and introduces items and slots is called a continuity announcer.

cue 1) signal to the presenter to begin a new slot or action 2) to set music or other audio recordings in readiness to play

democratic country with a government elected by its people

digital radio waves that are converted into a computerized form for transmission, making them more stable and enabling more of them to be transmitted at one time

director a program coordinator (sometimes also acting as producer)

drive time the hours during which most people travel to and from work or school

fade when one sound is gradually made quieter to be replaced by another sound

fader slider on a radio console that brings sounds in, takes them out, and fades the volume up and down

fidelity accuracy of the balance achieved by a radio receiver when it amplifies the different frequencies

format the way a radio show is arranged in terms of content

freelance someone who works for different employers, usually on individual jobs or on a short-term basis

frequency pulse of a radio wave moving at a certain number of cycles per second

interference the disturbance of a sound signal; unwanted noise

intonation pattern rise and fall of a person's voice as he or she speaks

jingle short burst of music or song that is part of a commercial or that introduces a presenter or slot

libel   to broadcast untrue and damaging information about a person or organization

modulation   varying a radio wave so that it can carry sound

narrowcasting   broadcasting specialized programs for a particular interest group

network   group of radio stations that share programs

pitch   level of a person's voice, whether high, medium, or low

prime time   morning and early evening peak listening times

producer   program coordinator (sometimes also acting as director)

ratings   calculation of the size of the audience for each radio show

receiver   equipment that receives sound signals

revenue   income, or money

royalty   sum paid to an author, performer, or songwriter for each performance of a work or for each book sold

signature tune   tune that introduces a program or a slot

slot   1) scheduled item in a radio show—a contest, commercial, phone-in, etc. 2) space in a schedule to be filled with programs or other broadcasts

station manager   person in charge of a radio station's finances and day-to-day output

studio manager (SM)   radio station's technical supervisor

take   a recording

trailer   broadcast of a short section of a future program or item designed to encourage listeners to tune into it later

transmit   to broadcast a program

transmitter   equipment that produces, modulates, and sends out radio signals

two-way radio   radio sets with microphones that enable people to communicate with each other

voice-over   spoken part of a prerecorded commercial

waveband   range of wavelengths between two given limits, allocated to radio stations

Index